Losing

story by Jenny Alexander
illustrated by Steve Smallman

Every day Mouse went to see
Lucky after school.
Every day Lucky came
hopping up to see Mouse.
"You are a hoppy bunny!"
laughed Mouse.

But one day Mouse went to see Lucky, and Lucky did not come hopping up. He just lay in the corner of his hutch.

Mouse thought that Lucky was asleep.
"Wake up, Lucky," said Mouse.
But Lucky did not wake up.

Mouse took Lucky inside.
“He will not wake up,”
Mouse said to Mum.
Mum looked at Lucky.
She looked sad.

Jojo came into the kitchen.
“Is Lucky asleep?” said Jojo.
Mum said, “No. He is not asleep.
Lucky has died.”

“He can’t have died,” said Jojo.
“This morning I saw him hopping about.”
Mouse gave her Lucky to hold.
Then Jojo knew it was true.

Mouse was angry.
“It isn’t fair!” he said.
“We fed him every day.
We played with him.
We cleaned his hutch.”

"You did everything you could for him," said Mum, "but rabbits do not live for very long. It was just time for him to die."

“What should we do now?”
said Jojo and Mouse.
Mum told Jojo to get a box.
She told Mouse to get some hay.

They put Lucky in the box.
"He looks happy," said Mum.
"He liked hay," said Mouse.

“I know,” said Jojo. “Let’s put all the things Lucky liked in the box.”
Mum thought that was a good idea.
Mouse agreed.

Mouse found a carrot and a slice of bread.
Lucky liked bread.
Jojo got his little teddy from his hutch.
He liked his teddy.
They could not put his hutch in, so Mouse and Jojo made a picture instead.

Soon Dad came home from work.
Mouse and Jojo took him to see Lucky.

They went into the garden.
Dad dug a big hole.
Mouse and Jojo watched.
Pip wanted to help.

They put Lucky in the hole.
Mouse was crying.
Jojo was crying.
They were crying because
they were losing Lucky.

Pip was crying too.
He was crying because
Mouse and Jojo were crying.

Dad pushed the earth back into the hole.
"Let's make the grave look lovely for Lucky,"
said Mum.

They got a big stone.
Mouse put some little stones around it.
Jojo got Lucky's bowl.
She filled it with water and put some daisies in it.

The grave looked lovely.
"I feel a bit better now," said Jojo.
Pip felt better too.

Mouse did not feel better though.
"How can I ever be happy again?"
he said.

But that night, Mouse had a dream.
In his dream Lucky could talk.
Mouse asked him, "What is it like to die?"

Lucky hopped around.
"It's like a big hop!" he said.
"A big, big, big hop!"
Lucky hopped up, up, up into the sky.

In his dream Mouse felt happy.

"You are still a hoppy bunny!" he said.